Slo

For Two

50 The Best Vegetarian Slow Cooker Dump Dinners For Two

Holiday Dishes, Easy Dinners, And Essential Cooking Tips

By: Lillian McDonough

individual in the profession should be ordered.

Table Of Contents

Introduction

No time to cook? Do you have a young family and just find it hard to squeeze in time to be in the kitchen and prepare meals? Or have you just got married and want to spend more time with your better half rather than in the kitchen? The answer is simple – now is the best time to invest in a slow cooker.

This holiday season, give yourself the gift of convenience and freedom by purchasing a slow cooker. Christmas season is usually a busy time and you would have to prepare dishes requiring longer periods of preparing and cooking. Do not sacrifice your precious time by slaving yourself in the kitchen. Now is the perfect time to get a slow cooker and have this amazing kitchen appliance work to your advantage.

Slow cookers have been giving wives of today the leeway to a) first, dump everything into this ever reliable kitchen appliance, b) and finally, let dinner prepare itself. If this sounds good to you, then this book is for you. Gone are the days of wives spending most of their time in the kitchen just to give their husbands the best and healthiest dishes there is. You have gone through a lot of grocery shopping for your vegan ingredients and cooking for an hour or two in the kitchen do not do justice. Thanks to slow cookers!

Once you have purchased your slow cooker, all you need to do is spend 15 minutes first thing in the morning before leaving for work to prepare the ingredients and then leave the slow cooker to bubble away. When you come home after a hard day's of work, a meal will be ready and waiting. All you need to do is dish up! Magic, right?

The very principle of a slow cooker is that it cooks dishes slowly at a constant temperature. So even though it is turned on for 10 or 12 hours, it would still consume the same amount of electricity as a light bulb. If you are worrying about your electric bills, know that slow cookers are very economical and will not leave a big hole in your pocket.

To get to know more about this amazing kitchen appliance and the delicious recipes it can cook, keep reading from cover to cover. You sure will find a treasure out of this cookbook.

Thanks again for buying this book.

Chapter 1 – The Vegetarian Slow Cooking

People have their own favorite recipes that they like to cook for their family and friends and these can be easily adapted to your slow cooker. Imagine having the luxury to go somewhere else to finish your errands on a weekend or go to work while your slow cooker cooks for you.

If you are following a vegetarian lifestyle, you can easily dump the ingredients in your slow cooker only needing to sauté some of them for 10 minutes or less. Almost all the recipes you will find here are suitable for two people and are easy to follow with simple directions.

Preparation is Key

It will usually take 15 – 20 minutes to prepare your vegan ingredients for your slow cooker. This preparation time includes chopping, peeling, marinating, frying, grilling, baking, and boiling before everything goes into the slow cooker, and before it does all the hard work for you. And so as they say, preparation is a key ingredient of these vegetarian slow cooker recipes.

For vegetables: squashes and pumpkins can take longer to cook than meat in a slow-cooked casserole. The secret? Cut these kinds of veggies smaller than you normally would.

For vegan pasta: they can be cooked in a slow cooker but not as successful as you would do it in saucepan. If you really want it cooked in your slow cooker, vegan pastas can be added to the slow cooker 50 minutes before the end of the cooking time.

For rice: choose those rice varieties that have been partially cooked during the manufacturing process. Also, purchase those that have some starch removed so it will not be as sticky once cooked. If you are going to cook rice at a slow cooker, you would have to double the amount of water to be used except for risotto rice.

On Choosing the Heat Settings

Most slow cookers have three heat settings: off, low, and high. Some models also have the following: medium, warm, and auto settings. As a general rule in using slow cookers, the low setting will take cooking dishes such as curries, stews, casseroles, and tangines. On the other hand, the high setting will take over half of the cooking time of the low setting.

Consider the following guidelines:

Low setting:

-   Vegetable casseroles

- Chopped, diced, minced, and braises

- Rice dishes

High setting:

- Puddings and cakes

- Pates

The variety of slow cookers is vast. But there are basically three sizes:

For a family of two: a 1.5 litre slow cooker with a working capacity of 1 litre is recommended. This can be used by single people as well.

For family of four: a 3.5 litre slow cooker with a working capacity of 2.5 litres is recommended. This can also be suitable for couples wanting to eat half of the served dish and freeze the other half.

For family of six: a 5 litre with a working capacity of 4 litres is recommended. This is a good size for those who wanted to make large batches of dishes and freeze individual portions.

The choice is still yours to make.

If you are new to this kind of appliance, you might be asking how you are going to choose the best one.

For one, choose the size that will most suit your cooking needs. If you are just a family of two, say a newlywed and is just starting to build a family of your own, you may use the smaller version (a 1.5 litre slow cooker with a working capacity of 1 litre).

Second, the most versatile shape is the oval slow cooker. This will allow you to use bakeware and tools such as soufflé dishes, loaf tins, pudding basins, and more.

Finally, choose a slow cooker that has an indicator light that will signal that the machine is turned on.

Once you have finally decided on the best slow cooker to buy, it is important that you read the manufacturer's guidelines. Remove all the sticky labels from the outside and wash the ceramic pot. Among other things you would have to keep in mind are the following cooking tips:

- Check if the slow cooker you bought needs some preheating before using. Some slow cookers need to be preheated for 15 minutes, while there are those that heat very quickly.

- Always turn the base unit off before you remove the ceramic pot.

- Do not worry about the slight smell of burning when you use the slow cooker. It is just normal and it will not spoil the food.

- When done using, do not wash and clean at once. Allow the ceramic slow cooker to cool before washing with soapy water if you wanted to prolong the life of the slow cooker.

- Should you wish to reduce the juices while slow cooking, all you have to do is replace the lid, turn the heat settings to high, and cook for a further 30 minutes.

- The following directions you will find in this cookbook asks for covering the lid. This is written for a purpose because as the food cooks, steam condenses on the lid and drops back to the slow cooker pot helping to produce a seal between the pot and the lid. This seal is broken each time you remove the lid and would account for an extra 20 minutes cooking time to regain a single minute of lost steam.

- Remember that this ceramic slow cooker will be very hot during cooking time, so better use your kitchen gloves when you lift it out of the base.

- If you wanted to serve the food warm, you can always turn the heating setting to low. This will warm the food without soiling it.

For some cleaning tips, consider the following:

- Always make it a habit to switch the base unit off before taking the slow cooker pot out of the slow cooker.

- Never immerse the entire unit in water. Switch, unplug, and leave it to go completely cold. Wipe the inside with soft cloth, and the outside with damp cloth.

- As with any other cooking appliance, it is best to let it cool before immersing in hot soapy water. Leave it to soak for a while and wipe with soft cloth. Some would just load it in the dishwasher without a care. Although this is tempting and is really time consuming, but know that this would only lessen the efficiency of your slow cooker or worse, shorten its life span.

- Slow cookers are not suitable to load in the dishwasher. And even if it so, it would only take up too much space. So you better wash it by hand.

In finishing your dishes:

The question now is to thicken or not thicken? It is often necessary to thicken stews at the end of cooking time. This can be done the same way you would in a stove. You can try mixing the cornflour with cold water to come up with a smooth paste. Stir in the stew and heat until thickened.

When it comes to browning, remember that vegetables cooked in a slow cooker will not brown. So if an ingredient requires browning, fry in a pan first.

Finally, the good thing about slow cookers is that the pot can be popped under a preheated grill until the food turns golden brown.

To get the most out of your slow cooker and begin cooking your vegan recipes, here are some basic guidelines:

1. Prepare the recipe – there are recipes needing make-ahead preparations. So it is best to prepare everything at night so you can have your ingredients all ready for the next morning. Definitely no hassle on your end.

2. On using liquid – for optimal cooking, the slow cooker should be three-quarters full or halfway full. If your recipe would be needing the use of liquid, it should be about halfway up or less the ingredients. Since very little liquid will evaporate from your slow cooker, you generally do not need a lot of liquid at all.

3. The safest spot to put the slow cooker – It is safe to leave your slow cooker unattended while it cooks meals for you, but a few safety precautions would not hurt. Position your slow cooker six inches away from other cooking appliances, walls, and kitchen utensils so heat can dissipate. Also, make sure that it is sturdy enough so your pet (if you have one) will not accidentally walk into it. No need to worry about the bottom part since it is safe for any types of counter top.

4. On setting the cooking time - the cooking temperature is similar as with all other settings, so your chosen setting would merely dictate how slow or quick your slow cookers achieve that temperature. Lower settings are usually 1 – 10 hours, while higher setting are usually between 4 – 6 hours. Modern slow cookers are now designed in bringing food to a temperature that is within a safe window and has the ability to hold it right there.

5. Walk away and let the slow cooker do the cooking – this is considered the true luxury of having a slow cooker. You do not have to wait in vain for hours and stand in the kitchen. You do not need to check the cooking progress from time to time. In fact, doing so will only hamper

the process of cooking and let the heat escape. So, if you are a busy woman feeding a family of two or more, the slow cooker is truly the answer to your kitchen and cooking needs.

6. The end of cooking time – But all because your slow cooker will do all the cooking for you does not mean you just have to let it do all the job. Of course, you have to do your part as well. Before the end of cooking time, make sure that you are around. But you can always go for slow cookers with "warming" cycle if in case you are not there when the dish cooks completely. It is a helpful feature but keep in mind that it could overcook the food when used for a longer period of time.

7. Doing it the slow pace is just great – use the low setting of the slow cooker as much as you can as most dishes bring out its natural flavors through slow cooking. Think of it as your cooking fairy – cooking wonderful and delicious dishes while you are out of the house.

8. How long is the cooking time as compared to cooking dishes in an ordinary stove?

For dishes that usually takes:

15 – 30 minutes, you can cook it in the slow cooker for 2 hours on high or 6 hours on low

For 30 minutes – 1 hour, you can cook it in the slow cooker for 3 hours on high or 7 hours on low

For 1 hour – 2 hours, you can cook it in the slow cooker for 4 hours on high or 8 hours on low

For 2 hours – 4 hours, you can cook it in the slow cooker for 6 hours on high or 12 hours on low

Note that root vegetables take more time to cook in the slow cooker than other vegetable variety and meat counterparts. Therefore, if it includes this kind of vegetable ingredient, put them at the bottom of the pot.

Chapter 2 – Slow Cooker Soups and Starters

Note: all the dishes can be cooked for a family of two. Should you have leftovers, it would not hurt to put them in the fridge to be eaten the next day.

Pumpkin Soup

Ingredients:

- 1 tablespoon olive oil

- 1 onion, chopped

- 1 kg pumpkin squash, cut into small chunks

- Fresh root ginger, grated

- 5 cups vegetable stock

- Pinch of salt

- Pinch of ground pepper

- 1 ripe tomato, chopped

- 1 cup coriander

- ½ small red onion, cut into wedges

- 4 tablespoons coconut cream

Directions:

1. Add the ingredients into the slow cooker and stir to combine well.

2. Add the vegetable stock and stir, scraping up some bits on the bottom of the pan. Cover with the lid.

3. Cook on low for 6 hours or until the pumpkin is tender.

4. Season to taste. Scatter with tomato, coriander, and onion. Drizzle with coconut cream.

Red Onion Soup with Goat's Cheese

Ingredients:

- 1 tablespoon olive oil

- 4 red onions, sliced

- 1 teaspoon sugar

- 1 tablespoon plain flour

- 4 cups vegetable stock

- 1 teaspoon thyme

- Pinch of salt

- Pinch of ground pepper

Directions:

1. In a bowl, put the oil and red onions. Sprinkle over the flour and gradually add stock. Stir constantly until well combined. Sprinkle over the thyme.

2. Carefully pour over the mixture into the ceramic slow cooker pot. Cover the lid and cook on high for 4 hours.

3. Season with salt and pepper. Ladle into a soup bowl. Arrange the goat's cheese on top pf the soup. Scatter thyme and drizzle a little olive oil. Serve.

Vegetarian Ricotta and Olive Pate

Ingredients:

- ½ cup olive oil

- 1 cup cashew ricotta cheese

- 55 grams vegetarian Parmesan cheese, finely grated

- ¼ cup applesauce

- 2 cups fresh breadcrumbs

- Pinch of salt

- Pinch of ground pepper

- 150 grams mint and lemon

- Mixed olives

- 8 sun-blush tomatoes

- Toasted slices of ciabatta

Directions:

1. Make ahead so you can just toss everything into the slow cooker (preferably the night before) – Line the base of a loaf tin with greaseproof paper. Check if the tin would fit into the base of your slow cooker. Oil the paper and sides of the tin.

2. Place the ricotta, parmesan, and applesauce into a bowl and blend until smooth.

3. Stir in the breadcrumbs and season with salt and pepper. Spoon into the tin and warp the loaf tin tightly with foil.

4. Put an upturned saucer into the base of the slow cooker and place the loaf tin on top. Pour the boiling water until it comes halfway up. Cover the lid and cook on low for 6 hours or on high for 3 hours.

5. Remove from the slow cooker and let cool. Scatter with olives and tomatoes. Serve with toasted ciabatta.

Spinach and Pea Soup

Ingredients:

- 2 tablespoons vegetable oil
- 2 teaspoons black mustard seeds
- 1 large onion, chopped
- 2 inches ginger, finely grated
- 1 green chilli, finely chopped
- 2 tablespoon s curry paste
- ½ teaspoon turmeric
- 3 ½ cups of water
- 1 ¾ cups coconut milk
- 1 cup frozen peas
- Pinch of salt
- Pinch of ground pepper
- 8 oz baby leaf spinach

Directions:

1. In a frying pan, heat the oil and add the mustard seeds. Sauté for 1 minute until the seeds pop.

2. Add the onion, ginger, chilli, curry paste, and turmeric and cook for 2 minutes.

3. Pour the boiling water into the pan. Put everything into the slow cooker together with the coconut milk. Add the peas.

4. Cover the lid and cook on low for 6 hours or on high for 3 hours.

5. Stir in the spinach and cook for another 10 minutes. Serve.

Lentil, Pepper, and Goat's Cheese Soup

Ingredients:

- 1 cup red lentils

- 1 onion, finely chopped

- 2 cups vegetable stock

- 2 tablespoon sun-dried tomato paste

- ½ cup soft goat's cheese

- ¼ cup applesauce

- Pinch of salt

- Pinch of ground pepper

- 1 yellow bell pepper

- Crisp crackers

Directions:

1. Rinse the lentils under cold running water and tip into the ceramic slow cooker. Add the onions, vegetable stock, and tomato paste. Cover the lid and cook on low for 4 hours or on high for 2 hours.

2. Remove the lentil and allow it to cool. Place into a bowl and add goat's cheese and applesauce. Beat until well combined. Season with salt and pepper.

3. Cover and cook on high for 1 hour. Drizzle with yellow pepper and serve with crackers.

Pumpkin Soup with Leeks

Ingredients:

- 2 tablespoons extra virgin olive oil
- 2 carrots, diced
- 2 stalks celery, diced
- 2 leeks, thinly sliced
- 4 cups vegetable stock
- Pinch of salt
- Pinch of pepper
- 4 cups pumpkin, cubed
- Chives

Directions:

1. In a pan, heat the oil. Add the carrots, celery, and leeks. Cook for 7 minutes. Add 2 cups of the stock and bring to a boil. Season with salt and pepper.

2. Transfer to the slow cooker and stir in the pumpkin and the remaining stock. Cover the lid and cook on high for 8 hours.

3. Puree using the blender and ladle into a bowl. Garnish with chives.

Leek and Pepper Soup

Ingredients:

- 2 tablespoons extra virgin olive oil

- 4 large leeks, thinly sliced

- 4 cloves garlic, minced

- Pinch of salt

- Pinch of pepper

- Tablespoon ground cumin

- 6 cups vegetables stock

- 4 medium sweet potatoes, cubed

- 2 green bell peppers, minced

- Chives

Directions:

1. In a pan, heat the oil. Add the leeks and stir for 5 minutes or until softened. Add the garlic, salt, pepper, and cumin. Stir for 2 minutes, Add 2 cups of the vegetable stock and stir well. Transfer to the slow cooker.

2. Add the remaining 4 cups of stock and the sweet potatoes. Cover the lid and cook on low for 6 hours. Add the green

peppers and season with salt and pepper.

3. Puree in a blender and ladle soup into bowls. Garnish with chives.

Coconut-Spiked Pumpkin Soup

Ingredients:

- 2 tablespoons extra virgin olive oil
- 2 onions, finely chopped
- 2 stalks celery, diced
- 2 carrots, diced
- 4 cloves garlic, minced
- 1 tablespoons ground cumin
- 2 tablespoons gingerroot, minced
- Pinch of salt
- Pinch of pepper
- 5 cups vegetable stock
- 6 cups pumpkin, cubed
- ¼ teaspoon cayenne pepper
- 2 tablespoons lime juice
- 1 cup coconut milk

Directions:

1. In a pan, heat the oil. Add the onions, celery, and carrots. Stir for 7 minutes. Add the garlic, cumin, ginger, salt, and

pepper. Add 1 cup of the stock and bring to a boil. Transfer into the slow cooker.

2. Add the remaining 4 cups of stock and the pumpkin. Cover the lid and cook on low for 6 hours. Puree in a blender.

3. Meanwhile, in a separate bowl, combine the cayenne and lime juice. Stir well and add to the slow cooker. Add the coconut milk, cover and cook on high for 15 minutes.

Christmas Cranberry Soup

Ingredients:

- 6 beets, coarsely chopped
- 5 cups vegetable stock
- 4 cloves garlic, chopped
- Pinch of salt
- Pinch of pepper
- 2 tablespoons coconut sugar
- 1 cup cranberries
- 1 orange juice
- 1 orange zest
- Vegetarian sour cream
- Dill fonds

Directions: In a slow cooker, combine the beets, stock, garlic, salt, and pepper. Cover the lid and cook on low for 6 hours.

1. Add the coconut sugar, cranberries, orange juice, zest, and beet leaves. Cook on high for another 30 minutes.

2. Puree in a blender and spoon into 2 individual bowls. Top with sour cream and garnish with dill.

34

Beet Soup with Lemon Grass

Ingredients;

- 2 tablespoons extra virgin olive oil
- 1 onion, chopped
- 3 cloves garlic, minced
- 2 tablespoons gingerroot, minced
- 2 stalks lemongrass, cut in half
- Pinch of salt
- Pinch of pepper
- 6 cups vegetable stock
- 6 beets, chopped
- 1 red chile pepper
- 1 red bell pepper, diced
- Coconut cream
- Cilantro leaves, finely chopped

Directions:

1. In a pan, heat the oil. Add the onion and cook for 3 minutes. Stir in the garlic, gingerroot, lemon grass, salt, and pepper, Add 2 cups of the vegetable oil. Stir well and transfer to the slow cooker.

2. Add the remaining stock and beets. Cover the lid and cook on low for 6 hours Add the red and chile pepper. Cook for another 30 minutes. discard the lemongrass

3. Puree in a blender and into bowls. Drizzle with coconut cream and cilantro.

Holiday Creamy Broccoli Soup

Ingredients:

- 2 cups almond milk

- 1 quart vegetable broth

- 1 small onion, finely chopped

- 1 package frozen broccoli

- Pinch of black pepper

- 1 cup vegetarian Parmesan cheese

Directions:

1. Blend together the milk, broth, onion, broccoli, pepper and 1 cup water in slow cooker bowl. Cover and cook on high for 3 hours or on low for 5 hours.

2. Toss the Parmesan Cheese into slow cooker until smooth. Serve immediately.

Yummy Carrot Soup

Ingredients:

- 1 onion, sliced

- 2 cloves garlic, sliced

- 3 carrots, cut into 3-inch pieces

- 2 cups water

- 1 vegetable broth

- 1 can coconut milk

- 2 tablespoons brown sugar

- 1 ground ginger

- Pinch of salt

- Fresh cilantro

- Chopped cashews

Directions:

1.   Put onion and garlic over the bottom of the slow cooker. Top with carrots. Add water and vegetable broth.

2.   Cover the lid and cook on low for 8 hours or on high for 6 hours.

3.   Uncover and stir in coconut milk, brown sugar, ginger, and salt. Puree until you reach the desired consistency.

4.   Transfer into soup bowls and garnish with cilantro and cashews.

Chapter 3 – Holiday Main Dishes

Holiday Stuffed Peppers

Ingredients:

- 1 tablespoons olive oil

- 1 cup herb stuffing mix

- 2 plum tomatoes

- 2 celery, diced

- Pinch of salt

- 5 red bell peppers, cored

Directions:

1. Combine oil and 3/4 cup of water in a microwavable bowl. Microwave for 1 minute. Add the stuffing mix and microwave for an additional 2 minutes. Stir.

2. In a bowl, combine tomatoes and celery. Stir until well blended. Add salt. Stir to combine.

3. Divide stuffing/mixture evenly among 5 peppers. Place into the slow cooker. Pour the boiling water until it comes halfway up. Cover and cook on low for 6 hours. Serve.

Vegetarian Baked Haricot Beans

Ingredients:

- 2 cups dried haricot beans, soaked overnight in cold water

- 2 large onions, chopped

- 1 carrot, finely diced

- 2 celery sticks, finely diced

- 2 teaspoon mustard powder

- Pinch of salt

- ½ cup brown sugar

- 1 bay leaf

- 2 cups passata

- 4 tablespoons tomato puree

Directions:

1. Put the soaked beans in a large saucepan and bring to a boil for 10 minutes. Drain and tip into the slow cooker.

2. Add the onions, carrot, and celery sticks.

3. In the same saucepan, put the mustard powder, salt, brown sugar, bay leaf, passata, and tomato puree. Bring to a boil. Pour the bean mixture into the slow cooker.

4. Cover the lid and cook on low for 8 hours or until the beans are tender.

Holiday Tomato, Spinach, and Goat's Cheese Cannelloni

Ingredients:

- 8 oz baby leaf spinach
- 1 cup soft goat's cheese
- Nutmeg, grated
- Pinch of salt
- Pinch of pepper
- Lasagna sheets
- Vegan mozzarella cheese, grated

Directions:

1. Rinse the spinach under cold running water and drain. Heat gently into a saucepan, no water, and heat until it wilts. Drain well.

2. In a bowl, put the spinach and stir in the goat's cheese. Season with nutmeg, salt, and pepper. Spread into the lasagne sheets and roll up tightly.

3. Pour half of the tomato sauce into the slow cooker and arrange the cannelloni over the sauce. Pour the remaining sauce.

4. Cook and cover on low for 3 hours.

5. Sprinkle over mozzarella cheese. Serve with salad leaves.

Chestnut and Veggie Sausage

Ingredients:

- 1 tablespoon olive oil

- 1 large onion, chopped

- 5 vegetarian Quorn sausages, cut into 3 pieces

- 1 lb chestnut mushrooms

- 1 large carrots, cut into chunks

- 2 tablespoons plain flour

- 1 tablespoon sage, chopped

- 2 ½ cups vegetable stock

- 1 tablespoon mustard

- 8 oz pack chestnuts

- Pinch of salt

- Pinch of pepper

- 1 courgettes, cut into chunks

- 1 cup cabbage, shredded

Directions:

1. In a large pan, heat the oil and sausages for 5 minutes. Add the mushrooms and carrots. Stir well for 4 minutes.

2. Sprinkle the flour and sage. Stir until all ingredients are well coated by flour. Put the stock and bring to a boil. Stir the mustard and chestnuts.

3. Put the mixture into the slow cooker and add the courgettes. Cover the lid and cook on low for 6 hours.

4. Add the cabbage and let it simmer for 5 minutes. Serve.

Veggie Chilli with Cornbread Biscuits

Ingredients:

- 1 tablespoon olive oil

- 1 large onion, cut into wedges

- 1 red bell peppers, cut into chunks

- 2 garlic cloves, crushed

- 1 large zucchini, cut into chunks

- 2 teaspoons chili powder

- 2 tablespoon plain flour

- 1 ½ cups vegetable stock

- 2 tablespoons tomato puree

- 14 oz canned tomatoes, chopped

- Pinch of salt

- Pinch of pepper

- 14 oz, canned red kidney

- 1 cup sweetcorn

Directions:

1. In a frying pan, heat the oil and sauté the onion for 4 minutes. Add the bell peppers, garlic, zucchini, and chilli powder. Stir for 4 minutes.

47

2. Put the flour and stir in the vegetable stock. Pour in the tomato puree and chopped tomatoes. Bring to a boil. Transfer the mixture to the slow cooker. Cover the lid and cook on low for 4 hours or on low for 3 hours.

3. Season with salt and pepper. Add the kidney beans and sweetcorn. Let it simmer for 10 minutes. Serve.

Holiday Vegetable and Fruits Stew

Ingredients:

- 2 tablespoons olive oil

- 2 teaspoon garlic, minced

- 2 fat red chilies, deseeded

- 1 large red pepper, cut into chunks

- 2 teaspoons ginger, minced

- 1 teaspoon ground turmeric

- 1 teaspoon ground cumin

- 1 teaspoon ground coriander

- 14 oz canned tomatoes, chopped

- 2/3 cup vegetable stock

- 2 tablespoons mango chutney

- 2 oz dried apricots, quartered

- 8 oz green beans, trimmed

- 2 cups cashew nuts, roasted

- Brown rice

Directions:

1. In a large frying pan, heat the oil. Stir in the garlic, chilies, red pepper, and ginger. Stir and cook for 2 minutes.

2. Add the ground spices, tomatoes, stock, mango chutney, apricots, and beans. Bring to a boil.

3. Transfer everything to the slow cooker. Cover the lid and cook on low for 6 hours or on low for 3 hours.

4. Scatter the cashew nuts over the stew and serve with brown rice.

Veggies with Garlic Bread Vegan Baguette

Ingredients:

- 2 tablespoons olive oil
- 1 onion, chopped
- 1 small eggplant, cut into chunks
- 1 red bell pepper, cut into chunks
- 1 yellow bell pepper, cut into chunks
- 2 courgettes, cut into chunks
- 4 garlic cloves, crushed
- 14 oz canned tomatoes
- 2 tablespoons plain flour
- 1 cup vegetable stock
- Parsley leaves, chopped
- 1 vegetarian baguette
- 2/3 cup pitted black olives
- 2 tablespoons pesto
- Pinch of salt
- Pinch of pepper

Directions:

1. In a frying pan, heat the oil. Toss the onion, eggplant, and bell peppers for 5 minutes. Add the courgettes and the garlic. Cook for 3 minutes.

2. Pour over the tomatoes, flour, and vegetable stock. Bring to a boil. Transfer the mixture into the slow cooker. Cover the lid and cook on low for 6 hours or on high for 3 hours.

3. Stir in the olives and pesto into the vegetables. Season with salt and pepper. Serve the veggies with garlic baguette.

Vegan Risotto with Peas

Ingredients:

- 2 tablespoons olive oil
- 1 garlic clove, crushed
- 2 fennel bulbs, finely chopped
- lemon rind, finely grated
- lemon juice
- 1 ½ cup vegan risotto rice
- 5 cups vegetable stock
- 1 cup frozen peas
- Pinch of salt
- Pinch of pepper
- Vegetarian parmesan cheese

Directions:

1. In a frying pan, heat the oil. Fry the garlic, and fennel bulbs. Stir in the rind and juice for 5 minutes. Stir occasionally or until the fennel begins soften.

2. Pour in the rice and vegetable stock. Bring to a boil. Transfer everything to the slow cooker. Cover the lid and cook on high for 4 hours or on low for 2 hours.

3. Stir in the peas and let it simmer for another 30 minutes. Season with salt and pepper. Serve with scattered Parmesan cheese.

Vegetable Curry

Ingredients:

- ¾ cup red lentils
- 1 large onion, finely chopped
- Handful of curry leaves
- 2 red chilies
- ½ teaspoon ground turmeric
- ½ teaspoon ground coriander
- ½ teaspoon cumin
- 2 teaspoon garlic, minced
- 1 teaspoon black onion seeds
- 2 teaspoon ginger, minced
- 3 cups vegetable stock
- 14 oz canned tomatoes
- 1lb small cauliflower florets
- Pinch of salt
- Pinch of pepper
- 6 oz baby leaf spinach
- 2 large tomatoes, cut into wedges
- Handful of coriander leaves

Directions:

1. Rinse the lentils in cold running water and put into the slow cooker.

2. Meanwhile, in a frying pan, heat the oil. Add the onion, curry leaves, and red chilies. Stir in the ground spices, cumin, garlic, and onion seeds. Stir for 3 minutes.

3. Add the stock and tomatoes and bring to a boil. Pour the mixture over the lentils. Stir in the cauliflower. Cover the lid and cook on low for 6 hours or on high for 3 hours.

4. Season with salt and pepper. Add the spinach and let it simmer. Sprinkle with chopped tomatoes and coriander. Serve.

Christmas Pumpkin and Red Bean Curry

Ingredients:

- 1 tablespoon olive oil
- 2 tablespoon red curry paste
- 1 onion, finely chopped
- 2 green chilies, thinly sliced
- 2 teaspoon ginger, minced
- 1 lb pumpkin, cubed
- 2 red bell peppers, cut into chunks
- 2/3 cup vegetable stock
- 1 ¼ cup coconut milk
- 125 g sugar snap peas
- 1 tablespoon soft brown sugar
- 14 oz canned aduki beans
- 1 lemon grind, finely grated
- 1 lemon juice
- 4 oz baby leaf spinach
- Handful of coriander

Directions:

1. Heat the oil in a frying pan. Stir in the curry paste and fry for 1 minute. Add the onion, chilies, ginger, pumpkin, and red bell peppers. Fry and stir occasionally for 5 minutes,

2. Add the vegetable stock and coconut milk and bring to a boil. Tip the mixture into the slow cooker. Cover the lid and cook on ow for 8 hours.

3. Stir in the snap peas, brown sugar, aduki beans, lime rind and juice. Cover and cook for another 30 minutes,.

4. Toss in the spinach and coriander and serve immediately.

Moroccan Vegetable

Ingredients:

- 2 tablespoons olive oil
- 1 large onion, cut into thin wedges
- 2 carrots, diced
- 1 lb butternut squash, cut into small chunks
- 2 teaspoon garlic, minced
- 1 large courgettes
- 2 teaspoon ginger, minced
- 1 teaspoon ground turmeric
- 1 tablespoon harissa paste
- 1 large red bell pepper, diced
- 14 oz canned tomatoes, chopped
- 1 ¼ cups vegetable stock
- Pinch of salt
- Pinch of pepper
- 14 oz canned chickpeas
- 4 ½ oz baby spinach
- 2 tablespoon maple syrup
- Handful of coriander

- Handful of fresh mint

- Brown rice

Directions:

1. In a frying pan, heat the oil. Add the onion and saute for 5 minutes. Add the carrots and butternut squash and stir for 5 minutes.

2. Stir in the garlic, courgettes, ginger, turmeric, harissa, bell pepper, tomatoes, and vegetable stock. Season with salt an dpper and bring to a boil. Put the mixture into the slow cooker. Cover and cook on low for 7 hours.

3. Stir in the chickpeas, spinach, maple syrup, and half the coriander and mint. Serve on top of brown rice.

Holiday Lentil Madness

Ingredients:

- 1 cup red lentils
- 1 tablespoon olive oil
- Handful of curry leaves
- 1 large onion, finely chopped
- ½ teaspoon ground coriander
- ½ teaspoon ground cumin
- ½ teaspoon ginger, minced
- ½ teaspoon garlic, minced
- 2 ½ cups vegetable stocks
- 14 oz canned tomatoes, chopped
- 6 oz baby spinach

Directions:

1. Rinse the lentils under cold running water. Drain and place into the slow cooker.

2. Meanwhile, in a frying pan, heat the oil. Add the curry leaves and onion. Stir for 3 minutes. Add the ground ingredients, ginger, and garlic. Stir for 5 minutes.

3. Add the stocks and tomatoes, then bring to a boil. Pour the mixture over the lentils. Cover the lid and cook on low for 6 hours.

Fennel Braised with Tomatoes

Ingredients:

- 2 tablespoons extra virgin olive oil
- 4 fennel bulbs, thinly sliced
- 1 onion, thinly sliced
- 3 cloves garlic, minced
- Pinch of salt
- Pinch of pepper
- 1 can diced tomatoes with juice
- Fennel fronds

Directions:

1. In a pan, heat the oil. Add the fennel bulbs and onion. Toss and cook for 5 minutes. Add the garlic, salt, and pepper. Continue stirring for 1 minute. Add the tomatoes with juice and bring to a boil.

2. Transfer to the slow cooker. Cover the lid and cook on low for 6 hours. Garnish with fennel fronds.

Holiday Butternut Squash in Coconut Milk

Ingredients:

- 6 cups butternut squash
- 1 tablespoon extra-virgin olive oil
- 1 onion, finely chopped
- 1 teaspoon coconut sugar
- Pinch of salt
- Pinch of pepper
- ½ cup vegetable stock
- 3 tablespoons coconut milk
- 1 tablespoon thyme leaves

Directions:

1. Put the butternut squash in the slow cooker.

2. In a pan, heat the oil and stir in the onions. Cook for 3 minutes. Add the coconut sugar, salt, pepper. Stir for 1 minute, add the vegetable stock and bring to a boil.

3. Transfer to the slow cooker. Cover the lid and cook on high for 6 hours. Using a

spoon, mash the squash and stir in the coconut milk and thyme. Serve hot.

Parsnip and Carrot Puree

Ingredients:

- 4 cups parsnips

- 1 teaspoon ground cumin

- 2 cups carrots, thinly sliced

- 2 tablespoons extra virgin olive oil

- Pinch of salt

- Pinch of pepper

- 1 teaspoon coconut sugar

- ¼ cup vegetable stock

Directions:

1. In a slow cooker, combine the parsnips, cumin, carrots, oil. Salt, pepper, coconut sugar, and vegetable stock. Cover the lid and cook on low for 6 hours.

2. Puree in a blender until smooth. Serve immediately.

Braised Sweet Onions in Balsamic Vinegar and Oil

Ingredients:

- 6 sweet onions, quartered
- 1 tablespoon extra-virgin olive oil
- 2 tablespoons balsamic vinegar
- Pinch of salt
- Pinch of pepper
- 2 tablespoon extra-virgin olive oil
- Parsley, finely chopped

Directions:

1. In a slow cooker, combine the onions, oil, vinegar, salt, and pepper. Toss until well-combined. Sprinkle some more oil.

2. Cover the lid and cook on low for 6 hours. Garnish with parsley.

Tofu in Mushroom Onion Gravy

Ingredients:

- 1 cup water
- 1 package dried porcini mushrooms
- 2 tablespoons olive oil
- 14 oz tofu
- 3 onions, thinly sliced
- 2 cloves garlic, minced
- 1 bay leaf
- 1 teaspoon dried thyme
- Pinch of salt
- Pinch of pepper
- 1 tablespoon tomato paste
- ½ cup dry sherry
- 8 oz cremini mushrooms, sliced

Directions:

1. Prepare ahead: In a bowl, combine water and mushrooms. Let it sit for 30 minutes.

2. Pat the mushrooms dry using a paper towel and chop. Reserve the liquid. Set aside both liquid and mushroom.

3. In a skillet, heat the oil and add the tofu. Stir for 4 minutes. Transfer to the slow cooker.

4. Add the onions, garlic, bay leaf, thyme, salt, pepper, and the reserved mushrooms. Stir in tomato paste. Add the sherry and the reserved liquid. Bring to a boil.

5. Transfer everything to the slow cooker. Stir in the cremini mushrooms. Cover the lid and cook on low for 8 hours. Discard the bay leaf.

Coconut Tempeh Curry

Ingredients:

- 2 tablespoon extra-virgin olive oil
- 1 lb tempeh
- 2 onions, finely chopped
- 3 cloves garlic, minced
- 2 teaspoon ground coriander
- 1 teaspoon ground cumin
- 1 teaspoon ground turmeric
- 2 tablespoons gingerroot, minced
- Pinch of salt
- Pinch of pepper
- 2 black cardamom pods, crushed
- 1 cinnamon stick
- 1 cup vegetable stock
- 1 cup coconut milk
- 1 teaspoon Dijon mustard
- 2 long red chiles, minced
- Cilantro, chopped

Directions:

1. In a pan, heat the oil. Add the tempeh and stir for 5 minutes or until light brown. Transfer to the slow cooker.

2. Add the remaining oil and cook the onions for 4 minutes. Toss in the garlic, coriander, cumin, turmeric, gingerroot, salt, pepper, cardamom pods, cinnamon stick and cook for 1 minute. Add the stock and bring to a boil.

3. Transfer to the slow cooker. Cover the lid and cook on low for 8 hours.

4. In a small bowl, combine the coconut milk, mustard, and chiles. Stir into the tempeh. Cover the lid and cook for another 30 minutes, Garnish with cilantro.

Chapter 4 – Easy to Prepare Side Dishes

Braised olive, fennel, and Parmesan

Ingredients:

- 4 medium fennel bulbs

- 1 lemon juice

- 1 lemon grind, grated

- 1 tablespoon olive oil

- 2 tablespoons tomato puree

- 14 oz canned tomatoes, chopped

- 2 tablespoons sugar

- 12 black olives

- ½ cup vegetarian Parmesan cheese

- Wheat crusty bread

Directions:

1. Trim the fennel and take away any discolored parts from its base. Slice thinly and toss in the lemon juice. Scatter in the base of the slow cooker.

2. Add in the lemon rind, olive oil, tomato puree, tomatoes, sugar, and olives Cover the lid and cook on high for 5 hours.

3. Scatter with vegetarian parmesan and let it melt. Serve with wheat crusty bread.

Chickpea and Eggplant Pilaff

Ingredients:

- 3 tablespoons olive oil
- 1 large onion, finely chopped
- 2 teaspoons garlic, minced
- 1 medium eggplant, cut into small cubes
- 1 cinnamon stick
- 2 teaspoons ginger, 2 cardamom pods
- 2 bay leaves
- Large pinch saffron threads
- 4 cups vegetable stock
- 3 oz dried apricots
- 1 cup brown rice
- 1 tablespoon tomato puree
- 1 cup raisins
- 14oz canned chickpeas
- 5 oz cherry tomatoes
- Pinch of salt
- Pinch of pepper
- Handful of coriander
- Lime wedges

74

Directions:

1. In a frying pan, heat 1 tablespoon of oil and stir in the onions for 3 minutes. Add the remaining oil and put the garlic, eggplant, cinnamon stick, ginger, cardamom, and bay leaves. Sauté for 5 minutes.

2. Add the saffron and stock. Stir in the apricots, brown rice, tomato puree, raisins, chickpeas, and cherry tomatoes. Bring to a boil.

3. Transfer to the slow cooker. Cover the lid and cook for 4 hours on low. Discard the cinnamon stick and season with salt and pepper. Sprinkle with fresh coriander and lime wedges.

Holiday Stuffed Bell Peppers

Ingredients:

- 1 large yellow bell pepper
- 1 large red bell pepper
- Pinch of salt
- Pinch of pepper
- ½ cup couscous
- 1 cup vegetable stock
- 4 oz cherry tomatoes, halved
- 1/3 cup pine nuts
- 2 oz raisins
- 2 tablespoons green pesto
- ½ cup vegan feta cheese
- Fresh basil leaves

Directions:

1. Cut the bell peppers half lengthways. Remove the core and seeds and the stalk in place. Season with salt and pepper.

2. In a bowl, pour the couscous and the vegetable stock. Set aside for 7 minutes.

3. Add the cherry tomatoes, pine nuts, raisins, green pesto, and feta cheese. Stir well to combine. Divide between bell peppers.

4. Put the bell peppers on the slow cooker and add the remaining stock on the peppers. Cover the lid and cook on low for 4 hours. Serve with scattered fresh basil.

Braised Celery with Cardamom and Orange

Ingredients:

- 2 celery hearts
- 1 orange juice
- 2 tablespoons sugar
- 1 tablespoon sweet sherry
- 1 teaspoon ground cardamom
- 14 oz canned tomatoes, chopped
- Pinch of salt
- Pinch of pepper
- 1 orange rind
- 1 cup fresh bread crumbs
- Handful of parsley
- ½ teaspoon olive oil

Directions:

1. Cut the celery in half lengthways. Get rid of any discolored ones, Place them at the bottom of the slow cooker.

2. Mix together the orange juice, sugar, sweet sherry, cardamom, and tomatoes.

Cover the lid and cook on high for 5 hours.

3. Drain the juices into a saucepan and let it boil for 5 minutes. Season to taste. Mix the orange rind, bread crumbs, parsley, and olive oil.

Puy Lentil

Ingredients:

- 1 tablespoon olive oil
- 1 red bell pepper, cut into chunks
- 1 yellow red bell peppers, cut into chunks
- 1 large red onion, cut into wedges
- 2 cloves garlic, crushed
- 1 bay leaf
- 2 tablespoons thyme leaves
- 14 oz canned tomatoes
- 1 1 /2 cup vegetable stock
- 1 cup Puy lentils
- 1 tablespoon sugar
- 3 tablespoons tomato puree
- 5 oz baby plum tomatoes
- Handful of parsley, chopped
- Pinch of salt
- Pinch of pepper

Directions:

1. Heat the oil and fry the peppers and onion for 5 minutes.

2. Stir in the garlic, bay leaf, thyme, tomatoes, stock, lentils, sugar, and tomato puree. Bring to a boil.

3. Stir in the plum tomatoes and scatter the parsley Season with salt and pepper. Cover the lid and cook on low for 6 hours.

Baked Onions and Sun-dried Tomatoes

Ingredients:

- 2 large onions

- 2 oz dried bread crumbs

- 2 tablespoons sun-dried tomato paste

- 6 sun-blushed tomatoes in oil

- 1 clove garlic, crushed

- 4 large basil, shredded

- Pinch of salt

- Pinch of pepper

- 2/3 cup vegetable stock

Directions:

1. Bring a pan to a boil and add the whole onions in their skins. Boil for 10 minutes. Drain and allow to cool.

2. Once cooled, peel the onions. Cut them in half horizontally. Scoop the center and leave a shell of at least 3 layers. Chop the scooped out onions and place in a bowl.

3. Add the bread crumbs, tomato paste, sun-blushed tomatoes, garlic, basil, salt,

and pepper. Spoon the stuffing into the onions.

4. Put into the slow cooker and pour the stock around the onions. Cook on low for 5 hours. Serve.

Chapter 5 – Yummy Holiday Slow Cooker Desserts and Preserves

Christmas Baked Apples

Ingredients:

- ½ cup dried cranberries

- ½ cup walnuts, chopped

- 1 teaspoon orange zest, grated

- 2 tablespoon coconut sugar

- 10 apples, cored

- 1 cup pomegranate juice

Directions:

1. I a large bowl, combine cranberries, walnuts, orange zest, and coconut sugar.

2. To stuff the apples and tightly pack core space with filling.

3. Place filled apples in the slow cooker. Cover the lid and cook on low for 6 hours.

4. Transfer the apples in the serving dish and spoon juices over them. Serve hot.

Poached Quince

Ingredients:

- ½ cup water

- ½ cup maple syrup

- 1 orange zest

- 5 quinces, sliced

- Coconut whipped cream

- 1 cup walnuts, chopped

Directions:

1. In a slow cooker, combine water, maple syrup, and orange zest. Toss in the quinces and stir well.

2. Cover the lid and cook on low for 8 hours.

3. To serve, top with coconut whipped cream and walnuts.

Red Plums with lemon Cream

Ingredients:

- 5 red plums, cut into chunks
- 1 cup cherries, pitted
- 1 cup strawberries, quartered
- Lime rind, grated
- 1/3 cup sugar
- 1 lime juice
- 2/3 cup almond cream
- 2 tablespoons lemon curd
- 5 sponge fingers
- 4 lime wedges

Directions:

1. Scatter the plums, cherries, and strawberries into the base of the slow cooker. Sprinkle with lime rind and sugar. Pour the lime juice.

2. Cover the lid and cook on low for 3 hours.

3. Whip the cream and add the lemon curd. Stir well.

4. Break up the sponge fingers and spoon over the fruit compote, top with lemon mixture. Put a lime wedge to decorate the glass.

Apricot and Pecan Nut Pudding

Ingredients:

- 2 tablespoons extra virgin olive oil
- ½ cup pecan, halved
- 1/3 cup dried apricots, halved
- 3 tablespoons maple syrup
- ¾ cup brown sugar
- 1 cup applesauce
- 1 orange rind, finely grated
- 1 ½ cup self-raising flour
- 1 orange juice

Directions:

1. Grease a pudding basin with oil. Scatter the pecan nuts and apricots in the basic. Drizzle over some maple syrup.

2. Meanwhile in a large bowl, combine the sugar and applesauce. Beat until creamy. Fold in the orange rind and flour. Mix until well combined. Pour in the orange juice. Spoon the mixture into the basin.

3. Oil a square greaseproof paper. Fold a pleat into the center and place it side down over the top of the pudding basin.

Cover with pleated foi. Cover the lid and cook on high for 5 hours.

4. Lift the pudding out of the slow cooker. Discard the foil and paper. Turn onto a serving dish.

Chocolate Espresso Cups

Ingredients:

- 1 ¾ cup almond milk

- ¼ cup vegan espresso

- 1 ¼ cup coconut cream

- Dark chocolate, broken into pieces

- 1 cup applesauce

- Large pinch ground cinnamon

- ½ cup sugar

- 2 amaretti biscuits

Directions:

Note: this can be prepared the night before it can be served.

1. In a saucepan, pour in the milk, vegan espresso, coconut cream, and dark chocolate. Stir and heat gently until the chocolate has melted.

2. Whisk the applesauce, cinnamon, and sugar. Gradually whisk in the chocolate mixture. Cover with foil and place on the slow cooker. Cover the lid and cook on high for 4 hours.

3. Lift from the slow cooker and chill overnight or for 3 hours if you are willing to wait.

4. When ready to serve. Chop remaining chocolate and scatter. Whip the remaining cream over amaretti. Serve immediately.

Ginger Crème Caramels

Ingredients:

- 2 tablespoons olive oil

- ¾ cup brown sugar

- ½ cup water

- 1 stem ginger, finely chopped

- 1 ¼ cup coconut milk

- 2 tablespoons maple syrup

- 1 cup applesauce

Directions:

1. Grease pudding basins with oil.

2. In a small saucepan, place the sugar and pour the water. Bring to a boil.

3. Divide the mixture between basins. Make sure the sides and base are coated with caramel.

4. Scatter the chopped ginger into the base of each pudding basin.

5. Pour the coconut milk, maple syrup, and half the stem ginger syrup into the saucepan. Whisk the applesauce in a large bowl the pour the milk mixture. Strain with sieve back into the saucepan.

6. Divide the milk mixture between the basins and cover with foil. Place in the slow cooker and pour in enough boiling water to come halfway up the sides of the basin.

7. Cook on low for 5 hours. To release the puddings, ease the edge of the custards away from the sides with a knife. Dip into hot water for 20 seconds. Turn upside down onto a plate and shake.

Ginger Cake

Ingredients:

- 5 balls stem ginger, sliced very thinly
- 2 tablespoons oil
- 1 ¼ cup sugar
- ¾ cup maple syrup
- 1 ¼ cups wholemeal self-raising flour
- ½ teaspoon baking soda
- 2 teaspoons ground ginger
- 1 cup applesauce
- 1/3 cup almond milk
- 2 tablespoons stem ginger syrup

Directions:

1. Line the base of a loaf tin with greaseproof paper. Arrange the stem ginger slices on to the base of the loaf tin.

2. Put the oil, sugar, maple syrup into a saucepan and heat gently. Stir until the sugar has dissolved. Remove from heat and leave to stand for 10 min minutes

3. Stir the flour, baking soda, ginger, applesauce, and milk into the golden

syrup mixture. Beat until well combined. Pour the mixture onto the loaf tin.

4. Cover the tin with plastic wrap. Place the tin in the slow cooker and pour in boiling water. Cover the lid and cook on high for 4 hours.

5. Carefully remove the tin from the slow cooker and let the cake cool. Remove from the tin and discard lining paper. Mix the stem ginger syrup and drizzle over the cake. Serve.

Lemon Poppy Seed Loaf

Ingredients:

- 3 tablespoons olive oil

- 1 ¼ cups brown sugar

- 1 cup applesauce

- 1 ¼ cup self-raising flour

- 2 tablespoons poppy seeds

- 3 lemons, unwaxed

Directions:

1. Line the base of a loaf tin with greaseproof paper.

2. Meanwhile, in a bowl, combine the oil, sugar, applesauce, flour, poppy seeds, and the zest of 2 lemons. Mix well. Pour in the loaf tin and cover with foil.

3. Put an upturned saucer into the base of the slow cooker and place the loaf tin on top. Pour enough boiling water so it comes halfway up. Cover the lid and cook on high for 3 hours.

4. Remove the tin from the slow cooker and discard the foil. Remove the cake from the tin while hot and discard the lining paper.

5. Shred the lemon rind and put in a saucepan with the remaining brown sugar and juice. Heat gently and pour the syrup over the cake. Leave to cool.

Cardamom Rice Pudding

Ingredients:

- ¾ cup pudding rice
- 1 lemon rind, finely grated
- 1 lemon juice
- 1/3 cup golden raisins
- 2 green cardamom pods
- 3 fresh figs
- 1 1/3 cup almond milk
- ½ cup maple syrup

Directions:

1. Place the rice into a sieve and rinse well under cold running water, Pour into the ceramic slow cooker. Stir in the lemon rind, juice, golden raisins, cardamom pods, and 1 litre boiling water. Cover the lid and cook on low for 3 hours.

2. Before the end of cooking time, preheat the grill and arrange the figs on a baking tray. Drizzle with maple syrup.

3. Stir the almond milk and remaining maple syrup into the rice pudding. Serve with figs.

Christmas Pudding

Ingredients:

- 1 tablespoon olive oil
- 1 cup self-raising flour
- 1 ½ cups white breadcrumbs
- 1 1.4 cup brown sugar
- 1 cup almond milk
- 1 cup raisins
- 1 cup currants
- 1 teaspoon baking soda
- 2 teaspoons mixed spice
- ¼ cup applesauce

Directions:

1. Grease a pudding basin with oil.

2. Mix the flour, breadcrumbs, brown sugar, milk, raisins. Currants, baking soda, mixed spice, and applesauce. Spoon into the basin. Cover with foil and tie a string handle over the top.

3. Lower the basin into the slow cooker. Pour enough water to come two-thirds up the side of the basin. Cover with lid and cook on high for 5 hours.

4. Lift the basin from the slow cooker and discard the foil. Put onto a serving plate. Serve.

Marmalade Pudding

Ingredients:

- 5 tablespoons olive oil
- 6 medium slices wheat day old bread, crusts removed
- 4 tablespoons marmalade
- 1 cup applesauce
- ¼ cup brown sugar
- 2/3 cup coconut cream
- 1 ¼ cup almond milk
- 1 teaspoons vanilla extract

Directions:

1. Grease an ovenproof dish with oil. Use the remaining oil to spread over the bread slices. Spread the marmalade over the slices of bread. And make a sandwich out of the remaining bread. Cut into quarters.

2. Meanwhile, mix the applesauce and sugar in a bowl. Pour the cream and milk in a saucepan and warm until just below boiling. Pour the milk over the applesauce mixture and whisk until well combined. Put the vanilla extract. Pour

over the bread and leave to stand for 15 minutes.

3. Put an upturned saucer into the base of the slow cooker and lay a foil on top of the dish. Lower the dish onto the ceramic slow cooker. Cover the lid and cook on low for 5 hours.

4. Carefully lift the dish out of the slow cooker. Discard the foil. Let cool for 5 minutes and serve.

Fruit Bowl Chutney

Ingredients:

- 1 lb tomatoes, roughly chopped
- 2 peaches, roughly chopped
- ½ cup raisins
- 2 apples, roughly chopped
- 2 red onions, finely chopped
- ¾ cup dried apricots, finely chopped
- 2/3 cup vegan malt vinegar
- 4 garlic cloves, crushed
- 2 teaspoons wholegrain mustard
- 4 tablespoons dark brown sugar
- 1 star anise
- Pinch of salt

Directions:

1. In a slow cooker, place the tomatoes, peaches, raisins, apples, onions, apricots, malt vinegar, garlic, mustard, sugar, star anise, and salt. Cover the id and cook on high for 6 hours.

2. In a food processor, place a ladleful of the chutney and whizz until smooth.

103

3. Spoon the chutney into the jar, cover with waxed disc and seal tightly with a lid. Store in the fridge. This will last for 3 weeks.

Vegan Barbecue Sauce

Ingredients:

- ¾ cup dried apricots, roughly chopped
- 1/3 cup raisins
- 1/3 cup sultanas
- 2/3 cup balsamic vinegar
- 5 tablespoons sherry
- 1 lb ripe tomatoes, roughly chopped
- 1 orange rind
- I orange juice
- Pinch of salt
- Pinch of pepper
- 2 tablespoons tomato puree
- 1 tablespoon Dijon mustard
- 3 tablespoons dark brown sugar
- 2 splashes Worcestershire sauce

Directions:

1. In a bowl, combine the apricots, raisins, and sultanas. Pour over the sherry and balsamic vinegar. Cover and soak for 4

hours. (Note: You may prepare this the night before).

2. In a food processor, pour the dried fruit and soaking liquid. Add the tomatoes, orange rind, orange juice, salt, pepper, tomato puree, mustard, brown sugar, and Worcestershire sauce, and whizz. Pour the mixture in a slow cooker. Cover the lid and cook on high for 6 hours.

3. Spoon the mixture into the jar, cover with waxed disc and seal tightly with a lid. Store in the fridge. This will last for 3 weeks.

Three Fruit Curd

Ingredients:

- 4 tablespoons olive oil
- 2 cups brown sugar
- Lemon grind
- Lemon juice
- Orange rind
- Orange juice
- Lime rind
- Lime juice
- 1 cup applesauce

Directions:

1. In a saucepan, heat the oil. Stir in the sugar and the rind and juice from lemon, orange, and lime. Whisk the applesauce with a fork into the lemony mixture. Cover the basin with foil.

2. Place the bowl into the slow cooker and pour enough boiling water to come halfway up the side of the pudding basin. Cover the lid and cook on low for 4 hours.

3. Spoon the mixture into the jar, cover with waxed disc and seal tightly with a lid. Store in the fridge. This will last for 3 weeks.

Conclusion

Thanks again for buying this book.

I hope this book has helped you with your cooking dilemma. Now with a slow cooker as your aid, you no longer have to worry about vegetarian dishes that you can serve for your significant other. Yes, cooking for two is easy, but it has never been this easier with the help of your slow cooker. You can just leave it in your kitchen as you prepare to go to work and come home to a cooked meal in the evening. Just remember to prepare the ingredients that need some overnight preparations. It is also important that you have a meal plan for the week. This way, you don't have to stress yourself thinking of what to cook next for your partner.

The next step is to share the recipes and cooking tips you have learned from this book to your friend, family, and coworkers. This is definitely one treasure you will proudly impart to the people you most care about. You can have this cookbook serve as a gift to your friends and coworkers or better yet give a slow cooker for your Mom or sister as a present this Christmas.

Finally, if you enjoyed this book, then I'd like to ask you for a favor, would you be kind enough to leave a review for this book on Amazon? It'd be greatly appreciated!

Thank you and good luck!

Made in the USA
Middletown, DE
26 December 2016